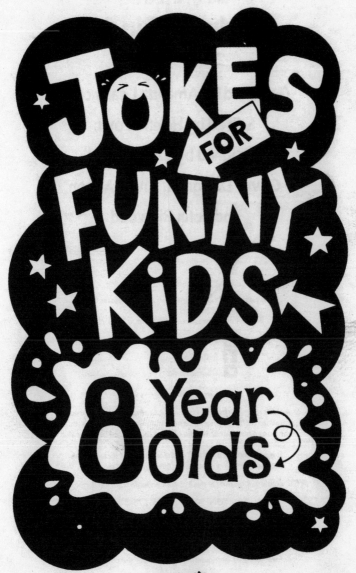

JOKES FOR FUNNY KIDS

8 Year Olds

Buster Boo

Illustrated by
Andrew Pinder

Compiled by Amanda Learmonth

Edited by Helen Brown

Designed by Jack Clucas

Cover Design by Angie Allison

and John Bigwood

First published in Great Britain in 2019 by Buster Books,
an imprint of Michael O'Mara Books Limited,
9 Lion Yard, Tremadoc Road, London SW4 7NQ

W www.mombooks.com/buster

f Buster Books

@BusterBooks

A CIP catalogue record for this book is available from the British Library.

ISBN: 978-1-78055-625-3

2 4 6 8 10 9 7 5 3 1

Papers used by Buster Books are natural, recyclable products
made from wood grown in sustainable forests. The manufacturing processes
conform to the environmental regulations of the country of origin.

Printed and bound in August 2019 by CPI Group (UK) Ltd,
108 Beddington Lane, Croydon, CR0 4YY, United Kingdom

MIX
Paper from
responsible sources
FSC® C020471

FSC
www.fsc.org

CONTENTS

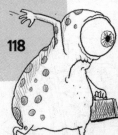

Introduction

Why do you like jokes about history?

Because they
are pre-hysterical.

Welcome to this te he he-larious collection
of the best jokes for 8-year-olds.

In this book you will find over 300 hysterical
jokes which will have you howling with laughter –
from funny characters and historical howlers
to tongue twisters and limericks.

If these jokes don't tickle your funny bone
then nothing will. Don't forget to share your
favourites with your friends and family
and practice your comic timing!

Monster
Mashup

Which monster is the brightest?

Franken-shine.

What do you get if you cross a Scottish monster with a bad egg?

The Loch Ness Pongster.

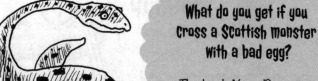

How do you greet a three-headed monster?

Hello, hello, hello.

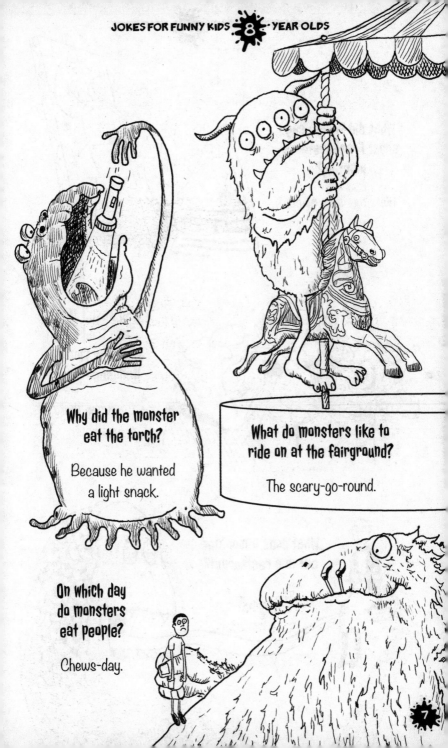

Why did the monster eat the torch?

Because he wanted a light snack.

What do monsters like to ride on at the fairground?

The scary-go-round.

On which day do monsters eat people?

Chews-day.

What did people say about Frankenstein's painting?

It's a monster-piece.

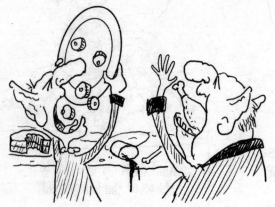

Why wasn't there any food left after the monster Halloween party?

Everyone there was goblin.

What does a monster eat in a restaurant?

The waiters!

How do monsters like their eggs?

Terror-fried.

What's big, hairy, dangerous and has four wheels?

A monster on a skateboard.

How does a monster begin a story?

Once upon a slime ...

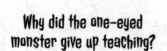

Why did the one-eyed monster give up teaching?

He only had one pupil.

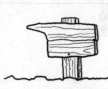

What do monsters love to play at parties?

Swallow the leader!

What kind of cheese do monsters like?

Monster-ella.

How do monsters keep their fur looking neat and tidy?

They use scare spray.

Why is the letter V like a monster?

It comes after U.

Knock Knock!

Who's there?

Butter.

Butter, who?

Butter run away, there's a monster behind you!

What kind of photos do elves like taking?

Elfies.

What do elves like to do in their spare time?

Watch the tel-elf-vision.

Why did the monster knit herself three socks?

Because she had three feet.

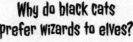

Why do black cats prefer wizards to elves?

Because they like sorcerers of milk.

What do you call a wizard with fur?

Hairy Potter.

What happened to the naughty wizard at school?

He was ex-spelled.

What do you call a fairy that won't take a bath?

Stinker-bell.

Who granted the fish princess a wish?

Her fairy cod-mother.

What's the difference between a carrot and a unicorn?

One's a bunny feast, the other's a funny beast.

14

What did the dragon say when he saw the knight in shining armour?

I hate tinned food.

What's big, scaly, breathes fire and bounces?

A dragon on a trampoline.

What's a dragon's favourite snack?

Firecrackers.

What sound do you hear when dragons eat spicy food?

A fire alarm.

Why do dragons sleep during the day?

So they can fight knights.

Why are dragons good storytellers?

Because they have such long tails.

**Why is a dragon
like a BBQ?**

They are always
smoking.

How do you compliment a dragon?

Tell it it's claw-some.

What do polite dragons say?

Fang you very much.

Brain Bogglers

What has hands but can't clap?

A clock.

I'm not alive, but I have five fingers. What am I?

A glove.

What begins with an 'e', ends with an 'e', has an 'e' in the middle, but has only one letter?

An envelope.

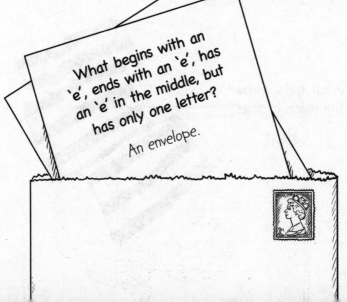

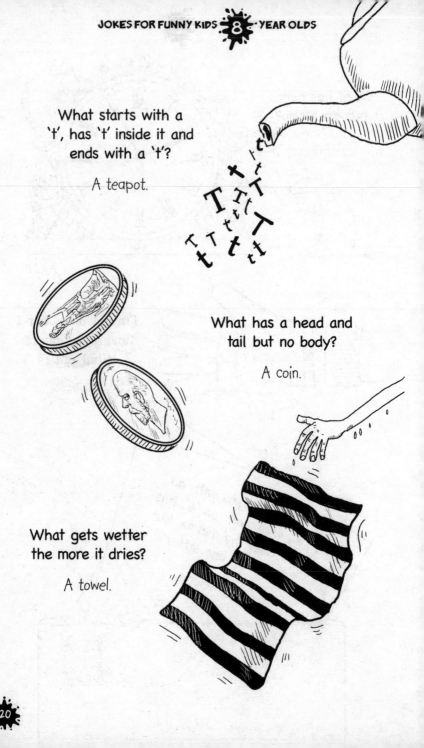

What starts with a
't', has 't' inside it and
ends with a 't'?

A teapot.

What has a head and
tail but no body?

A coin.

What gets wetter
the more it dries?

A towel.

A cowboy rode in to town on Friday, stayed for three days, then left on Friday. How did he do it?

His horse's name was Friday.

What comes once in a minute, twice in a moment, but never in a thousand years?

The letter 'm'.

What is at the end of the rainbow?

The letter 'w'.

What's full of
holes but still
holds water?

A sponge.

Tom's mother had four
children. She named the
first child Monday, the
second Tuesday, and
the third Wednesday.
What is the name of
the fourth child?

Tom, because Tom's mother
only had four children.

What can you hold
without touching it?

Your breath.

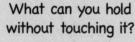

What goes up as
rain comes down?

An umbrella.

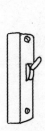

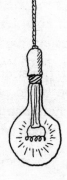

When I point up,
it's bright. When
I point down, it's
dark. What am I?

A light switch.

What has an eye
but cannot see?

A needle.

What has four
legs, two arms
but no head?

An armchair.

I travel around
the world but only
stay in one corner.
What am I?

A stamp.

What has 13 hearts
but is never alive?

A pack of cards.

I'm as hard as a rock but melt in hot water. What am I?

An ice cube.

I can hold lots of food, but I can't eat anything. What am I?

A fridge.

What clever invention lets you walk through walls?

A door.

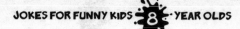

You have a bucket filled with sand. It is too heavy to carry. What can you put in your bucket that will make it lighter and easier to carry?

A hole.

What is more useful to you once its broken?

An egg.

If two cockerels lay three eggs a day for four days, how many eggs would they lay on the fifth day?

None. Cockerels don't lay eggs.

What weighs more – a kilo of potatoes or a kilo of balloons?

They both weigh the same - a kilo.

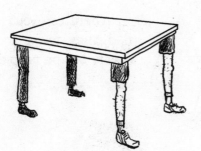

What has four legs but can't walk?

A table.

What's easy to catch but hard to get rid of?

A cold.

**What can run
but can't walk?**

Water.

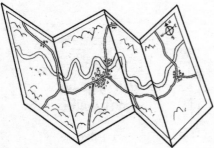

**Where can you
find cities, towns and
streets but no people?**

A map.

**What word is
spelled wrong in
every dictionary?**

The word 'wrong'.

You can see me in water but I never get wet. What am I?

A reflection.

Which month is the shortest?

May (it only has three letters).

I can go through glass without breaking it. What am I?

Light.

Holiday Humour

Knock Knock!

Who's there?

Wendy.

Wendy, who?

Wendy bell rings, school's out for summer.

Where do sharks like to go on holiday?

Fin-land.

Where do eggs like to go on holiday?

New Yolk City.

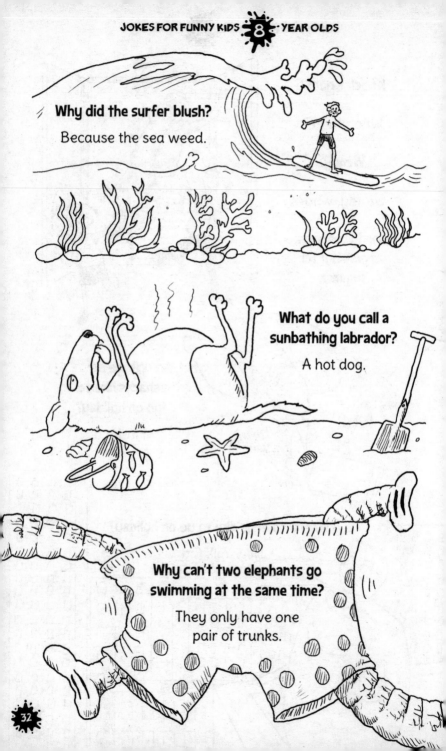

Why did the surfer blush?

Because the sea weed.

What do you call a sunbathing labrador?

A hot dog.

Why can't two elephants go swimming at the same time?

They only have one pair of trunks.

What do frogs like to drink on a hot summer's day?

Croak-a-cola.

What did one volcano say to the other volcano?

I lava you.

What do you call a snowman in hot weather?

A puddle.

What's brown, hairy and sleeps in a tent?

A coconut on a camping trip.

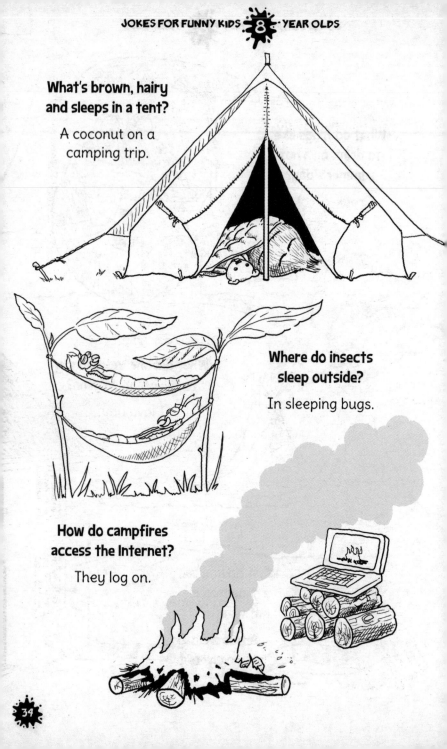

Where do insects sleep outside?

In sleeping bugs.

How do campfires access the Internet?

They log on.

What's the best day of the week to go camping?

Sun-day.

Did you hear about the climbers on holiday?

It's hill-arious!

Knock Knock!

Who's there?

Alpaca.

Alpaca, who?

Alpaca the bags, let's go on holiday.

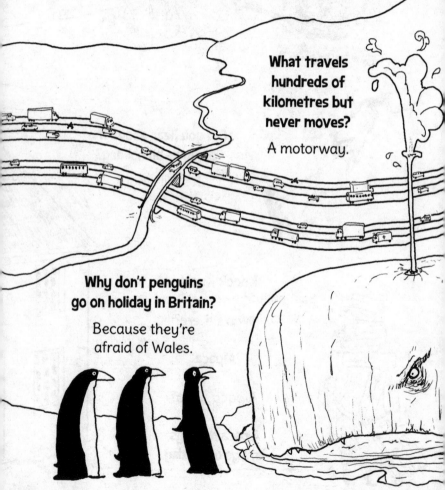

What flies, has a nose but can't smell?

An aeroplane.

What travels hundreds of kilometres but never moves?

A motorway.

Why don't penguins go on holiday in Britain?

Because they're afraid of Wales.

What wobbles when it flies?

A jelly-copter.

What do you get if you cross a dog and an aeroplane?

A jet-setter.

What happens when you wear a watch on a plane journey?

Time flies.

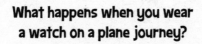

Knock Knock!

Who's there

Canoe.

Canoe, who?

Canoe row the boat faster, please?

Which vegetable should you never invite on a boat trip?

A leek.

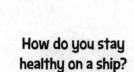

How do you stay healthy on a ship?

Take plenty of vitamin sea.

What do you call a train carrying bubble gum?

A chew-chew train.

What did the bicycle say as it raced down the hill?

This is wheelie fun!

I couldn't work out how to fasten my seatbelt ...

... then it clicked.

What do people eat for lunch on a skiing holiday?

Ice-burgers.

Where do sheep like to go on holiday?

The Baa-hamas.

Knock Knock!

Who's there?

Snow.

Snow, who?

Snow use, I forgot my name again.

Sophie: What did you do in Switzerland?

Ollie: I thought about going snowboarding, but then I let it slide.

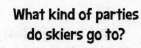

What kind of parties do skiers go to?

Snow-balls.

What did the police officer say when she saw the snowman stealing?

Freeze!

In which country can you never stop eating?

Hungary.

What is the fastest country in the world?

Russia.

What is the spiciest country to visit?

Chile.

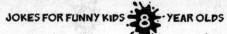

NEWSFLASH!

POLICE ARREST CHEF

They say he was caught
beating an egg.

WOMAN FORGETS TO BUY SOAP

"It slipped my mind,"
she claims.

WIGS STOLEN FROM WIGMAKER'S SHOP

Police are combing
the area to find it.

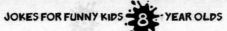

BUTCHER CHARGES TOO MUCH FOR MEAT

"I've clearly made a big miss-steak," he confesses.

ACTOR BREAKS THE FLOORBOARDS

Rumour has it that he's going through a stage.

MAN SHOWS HIS BELLY BUTTON IN PUBLIC

It is now under a vest.

JOKES FOR FUNNY KIDS 8 YEAR OLDS

NOW FOR THE WEATHER
It's so hot today ...

... Chickens are laying boiled eggs.

... Cows are giving
dried milk.

... The oven is lighting itself.

... The water sprinkler is
coming out as steam.

... The popcorn is
popping itself.

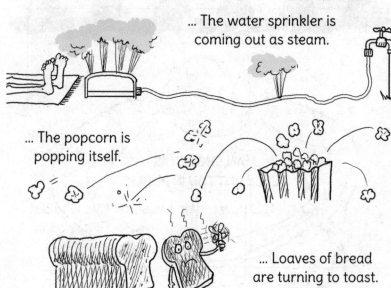

... Loaves of bread
are turning to toast.

46

It'll be so cold tomorrow ...

... Cows will give ice cream instead of milk.

... Pet shops will sell penguins.

... Cafés will serve coffee ice lollies.

... Polar bears will be buying fur coats.

... You'll need to open the fridge to heat the house.

... You'll have to put your skates on to go to the toilet.

Why should you be careful when it's raining cats and dogs?

You might step in a poodle.

Why isn't the sky happy on clear days?

Because it has the blues.

Why do hurricanes travel so fast?

If they didn't, they'd be slow-icanes.

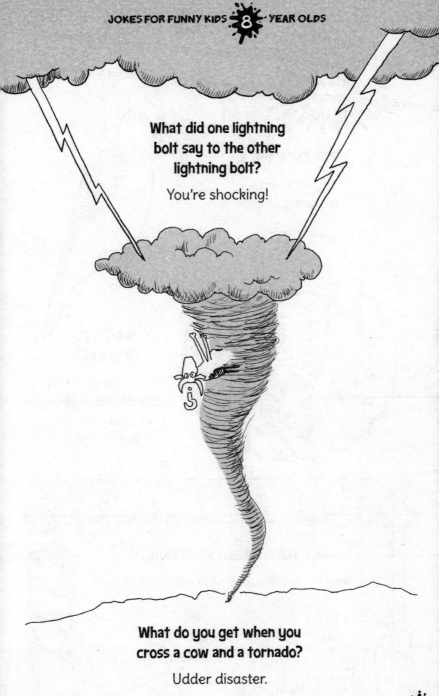

What did one lightning bolt say to the other lightning bolt?

You're shocking!

What do you get when you cross a cow and a tornado?

Udder disaster.

ADVERTISEMENTS

PET SHOP SALE

All the birds
are going cheep.

**WANTED:
BAKERS**

We knead you! You
dough-not want
to miss this job
opportunity.

GET YOUR FRESH VEGETABLES

Come in and lettuce know what you'd like.

WANTED: CHEESE MAKER

Must be a grate person who is very mature.

NEW WATER MAMMALS AT THE ZOO

We thought you otter know this seal-ly exciting news!

FOR SALE: CLOWNFISH

Do not eat – they taste funny.

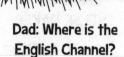

WHAT'S ON TV?

Dad: Where is the English Channel?

Son: I don't know, our TV doesn't pick up the signal.

What do you call a TV weather presenter?

Gale.

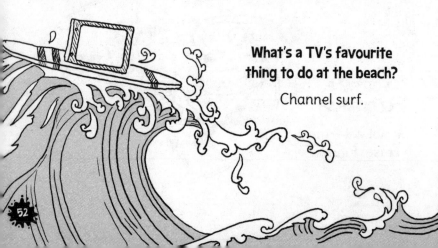

What's a TV's favourite thing to do at the beach?

Channel surf.

Son: I was on the TV last night!

Dad: Wouldn't you have been more comfortable on the sofa?

What do you call someone who watches TV all day?

Anything you like, they're not listening to you anyway!

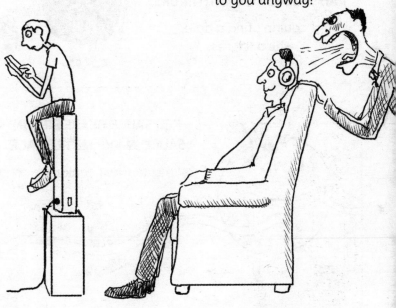

Mum: Shall I put the TV on?

Daughter: No, the dress you're wearing looks fine.

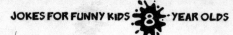
... AND FINALLY

RAISIN GOES OUT WITH PRUNE

"I couldn't find a date,"
she declares.

RED SAUCE BEATS BROWN
SAUCE IN 100-METRE RACE

Brown sauce just couldn't ketchup!

FARMER PLOUGHS FIELD
WITH A STEAMROLLER

"I wanted to grow mashed
potatoes," he explains.

FRENCH DISCOVERY

An interesting letter has been found in the centre of Paris: the letter 'R'.

ANIMALS ESCAPED FROM ZOO

One is a giraffe, the other is a mouse. The police are looking high and low for them.

DANCING DANGERS

A tap dancer has broken his ankle. Apparently he fell into the sink.

Funny Characters

How do we know that Rapunzel went to lots of parties?

Because she was always letting her hair down.

What do you call a snowman in the desert?

Lost.

What's Chewbacca's favourite treat?

Chocolate chip Wookies.

Why were there no horses to pull Cinderella's coach?

They were too busy playing stable tennis.

Which is a cow's favourite Disney character?

Moo-ana.

What do mermaids like on toast?

Merm-alade.

Why didn't anyone believe what the big cat said?

Because he was lion.

Knock Knock!

Who's there?

Tinkerbell.

Tinkerbell, who?

I 'Tink' your bell is out of order.

Which magical book do pigs like to read?

Harry Trotter.

What did the dog say to the flea?

Stop bugging me!

What are James Bond's favourite Christmas treats?

Mince spies.

Who stuck her tongue out at the Big Bad Wolf?

Little Rude Riding Hood.

What does Winnie the Pooh wear in bed?

Pooh-jamas.

What do you call Paddington Bear with a missing ear?

Paddington B.

Do you know what's inside Aladdin's lamp?

You'd need to be a genie-us to find out.

What happened when the rabbit won the lottery?

He became a million-hare.

What is Count Dracula's favourite fruit?

Neck-tarines.

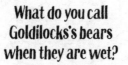

How does a blind mouse feel after he's had a shower?

Squeaky clean.

What do you call Goldilocks's bears when they are wet?

Drizzly bears.

Why did Goldilocks suffer such a bad night's sleep?

Because she had night-bears.

How did the dog feel when he sat on sandpaper?

Ruff.

How do the three little pigs write secret messages?

With invisible oink.

What does a dog use to wash his fur?

Sham-poodle.

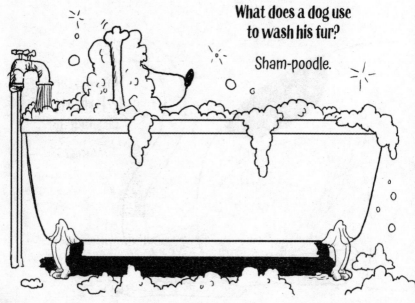

What do Harry Potter's best friend and his potion pot have in common?

They're both cauldron.

What is Postman Pat called on holiday?

Pat.

What do you call James Bond under water?

Bubble 07.

Knock Knock!

Who's there?

Aladdin.

Aladdin, who?

A lad in the street who wants to come in!

What did Cinderella say when her photos didn't arrive?

Some day my prints will come.

Historical Howlers

Which queen couldn't stop drinking water?

Elizabeth the Thirst.

Why were the early days of history called the Dark Ages?

Because there were so many knights.

What did Henry VIII do when he gained the throne?

He sat down on it!

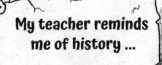

My teacher reminds me of history ...

... He's always repeating himself.

Knock Knock!

Who's there?

Queen.

Queen, who?

Queen your room, it's filthy.

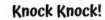

What did the executioner say to the prisoner?

I'm just trying to get ahead.

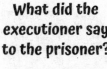

What's fruity and burns?

The Grape Fire of London.

Who invented fractions?

Henry the one eighth.

Why is England such a wet country?

Because kings and queens have reigned there for hundreds of years.

Where was Queen Elizabeth I crowned?

On her head.

Why does Guy Fawkes have the best birthdays?

His parties always go out with a bang.

Which queen burped a lot?

Queen Hic-toria.

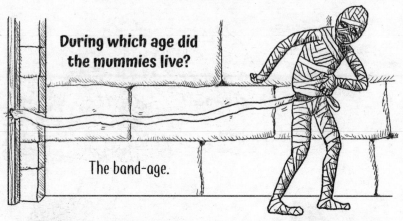

During which age did the mummies live?

The band-age.

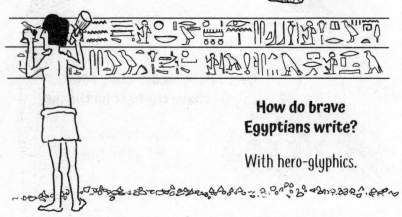

How do brave Egyptians write?

With hero-glyphics.

What do you get at the top of a 5-storey Egyptian pyramid?

A tomb with a view.

Do mummies enjoy being mummies?

Of corpse.

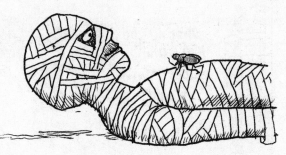

What did Caesar say to Cleopatra?

Toga-ther we can rule the empire.

What do Ancient Egyptians say when they hear the doorbell ring?

Toot-and-come-in (Tutankahmun).

75

What do you call a Roman emperor with a cold?

Julius Sneezer.

How was Caesar so good at drawing straight lines?

He was an ancient ruler.

What happened to the soldier who had his ear chopped off?

He was never heard of again.

What fish do Roman soldiers like to eat?

Sword fish.

How was the Roman Empire cut in half?

With a pair of Caesars.

Knock Knock!

Who's there?

Caesar.

Caesar, who?

Seize her! She's getting away.

Knock Knock!

Who's there?

Turner.

Turner, who?

Turner round, there's a pirate behind you!

Why can't pirates recite the alphabet?

Because they always get lost at 'C'.

How did the pirate get his ship so cheaply?

He bought it on sail.

What's a pirate's favourite letter of the alphabet?

'R'rrghh!

What did the pirate say as he walked the plank?

Water-way to go.

What do you call a pirate with four eyes?

A piiiirate.

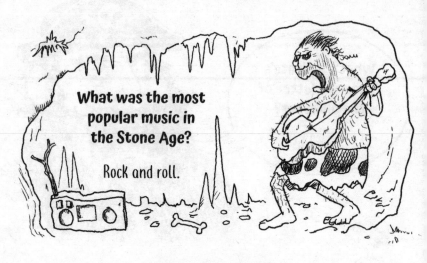

What was the most
popular music in
the Stone Age?

Rock and roll.

Why did the mammoth
have a woolly coat?

He would have looked
silly in a jacket.

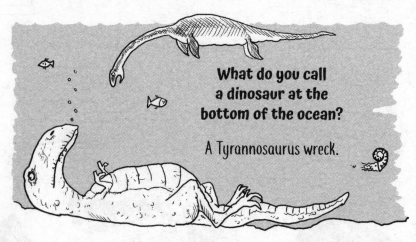

What do you call
a dinosaur at the
bottom of the ocean?

A Tyrannosaurus wreck.

Caveman 1: Why do we eat tortoises all the time?

Caveman 2: Too much fast food is bad for you.

In which period of history did no one's clothes have any wrinkles?

The Iron Age.

Why did King Arthur have a round table?

So he couldn't be cornered.

81

Jolly Jobs

What kind of job is it easy to stick to?

Working in a glue factory.

What did the lawyer name her daughter?

Sue.

How did the farmer mend the holes in his trousers?

With cabbage patches.

What kind of shoes do spies wear?

Sneakers.

What do you call killer whales playing the violin?

An orca-stra.

What do lawyers wear to work?

Law-suits.

Why did the book join the police?

He wanted to go under cover.

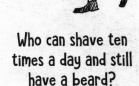

Who can shave ten times a day and still have a beard?

A barber.

Why are chefs cruel?

Because they whip the cream and batter the fish.

What do you get when you cross a teacher and a vampire?

Blood tests.

What vegetable do librarians like?

Quiet peas.

Shhh

How are judges like teachers?

They both hand out long sentences.

What time should you go to the dentist?

Tooth-hurty.

What was the name of the chef's son?

Stew.

What was the name of the chef's daughter?

Olive.

Why did the electrician hate his job?

Because it was shocking.

How do scientists keep their breath fresh?

With experi-mints.

Knock Knock!

Who's there?

Police.

Police, who?

Police open the door, it's cold outside!

88

Girl: My dog doesn't have a nose.

Vet: How does it smell?

Girl: Awful!

What do you call a dog that does magic?

A labracadabrador.

How do you train to be a waste collector?

You just pick it up as you go along.

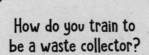

89

Why did the baker stop making doughnuts?

He just got tired of the hole thing.

What's yellow and white and travels at 100 kilometres an hour?

A train driver's egg sandwich.

Why are bakers so relaxed?

They're always loafing around.

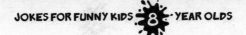
Who gets the sack
as soon as he
starts work?

A postman.

Why did the
farmer ride her
horse to town?

It was too
heavy to carry.

What kind of dance
does a plumber do?

A tap dance.

What's the difference between a composer and a postman?

One writes notes, the other delivers them.

Why did the ballerina quit?

Because it was tu-tu hard.

What did the rabbit want to be when he grew up?

A hare-line pilot.

Why were the swimmers so slow?

They could only do the crawl.

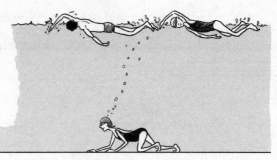

What does a cricket team and a pancake have in common?

They both need a good batter.

What did the artist draw before he went to bed?

The curtains.

What did one sheep say to the other?

I love ewe.

Why did the owl invite her friends over?

She didn't want to be owl by herself.

What did the pig farmer give her husband for Valentine's Day?

Hogs and kisses.

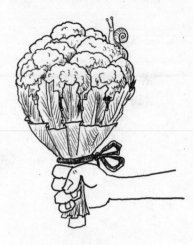

What kind of flower do you never want to receive on Valentine's Day?

A cauliflower.

What did the bat say to his friend?

It's fun hanging out with you.

What did the drum say to its sweetheart?

My heart beats for you.

What did one bee say
to the other bee?

I love bee-ing
with you.

Where do kittens buy presents
for other kittens?

From cat-alogues.

What did the baker
say to his wife?

I'm dough-nuts
about you.

Where do hamburgers go to dance with their friends?

Meat-balls.

Knock Knock!

Who's there?

Pooch.

Pooch, who?

Pooch your arms around me and give me a hug.

What did one cat say to the other cat?

You're purrr-fect for me.

Did you hear about the bed bugs that fell in love?

They're getting married in the spring.

What happened when the vampires went on a date?

It was love at first bite.

What did one orca say to the other orca?

Whale you be mine?

Why do squirrels never get married?

They'd drive each other nuts.

What do you call two birds in love?

Tweet-hearts.

How do animals that live underground send love letters?

By e-mole.

100

Anna: Do you have a date for Valentine's Day?

Millie: Yes, it's the 14th of February.

What did one sheep say to the other sheep?

Wool you marry me?

Boy: I love u.

Girl: Oh really?

Boy: Yes, it's my favourite letter.

Who loves to go to summer parties but is never invited?

Ants.

Did you hear about the shortsighted porcupine?

He fell in love with a pincushion.

Knock Knock!

Who's there?

Frank.

Frank, who?

Frank you for being my friend.

What flowers did the monkey get for Valentine's Day?

Forget-me-nuts.

Big sister: I can marry anyone I please.

Little brother: But you don't please anyone.

What did the calculator say to the pencil?

You can always count on me.

Boy: I can't leave you.

Girl: You love me that much?

Boy: It's not that. You're standing on my foot!

What did the envelope say to the stamp?

Stick with me and we'll go places.

Where is a wall's favourite place to meet its friend?

At the corner.

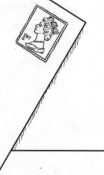

Knock Knock!

Who's there?

Keith.

Keith, who?

Keith me, thweetheart!

How do skeletons call their friends?

On the tele-bone.

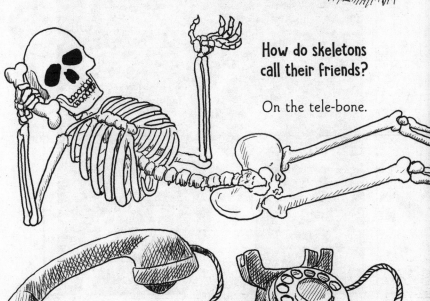

How do you propose over the phone?

Just give them a ring.

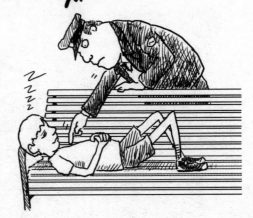

Did you hear about
the kidnapping in
the park?

They woke him up.

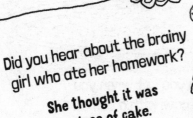

What's worse than one
crocodile coming to
dinner?

**Two crocodiles coming
to dinner.**

Did you hear about the brainy
girl who ate her homework?

**She thought it was
a piece of cake.**

Why did the man
run around his bed?

He was trying to catch
up on his sleep.

Why did the chickens
cross the road?

They thought it was
an egg-cellent idea.

What do you get when you
cross a cow with a camel?

Humpy custard.

Did you hear about the musical instrument found in the bathroom?

It was a tuba toothpaste.

What do you get when you cross a ghost with a kitten?

A scaredy cat.

What's the cleverest type of chocolate?

A smartie.

What is fast, loud and delicious?

A rocket chip.

Did you hear about the restaurant on the Moon?

The food is out of this world.

Why did the kettle get so hot?

It wanted to blow off steam.

What do you get when you cross
a snake with a builder?

A boa-constructor.

What do you call
two guys hanging
on a window?

Kurt and Rod.

Why did the
bacon laugh?

The egg cracked a yolk.

Why did the duck
cross the road?

**It was the chicken's
day off.**

How do you catch a
school of fish?

With bookworms.

What do you get when
you cross an elephant
with a bag of crisps?

Mashed potatoes.

What's the difference between school dinners and a pile of slugs?

School dinners come on a plate.

What do you get when you cross a cow with a grass cutter?

A lawn-mooer.

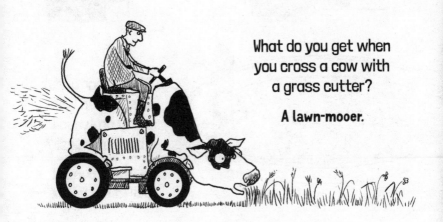

Did you hear about the man who put on a clean pair of socks every day a week?

By Sunday he could hardly get his shoes on.

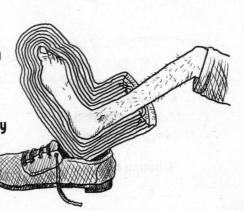

Why can't you trust
frogs with paper?

They rip-it.

Did you hear about
the woman who
nearly drowned in
a bowl of muesli?

**A strong currant
pulled her under.**

What do you get
when you cross a
rabbit with a frog?

A bunny ribbit.

What do you call
a man lying on
your doorstep?

Matt.

Waiter, Waiter! What
do you call this?

That's bean soup, Madam.

I don't care what it's
been. What is it now?

What happens when
you fill a suitcase
with toadstools?

**There's not mush-room
for your holiday clothes.**

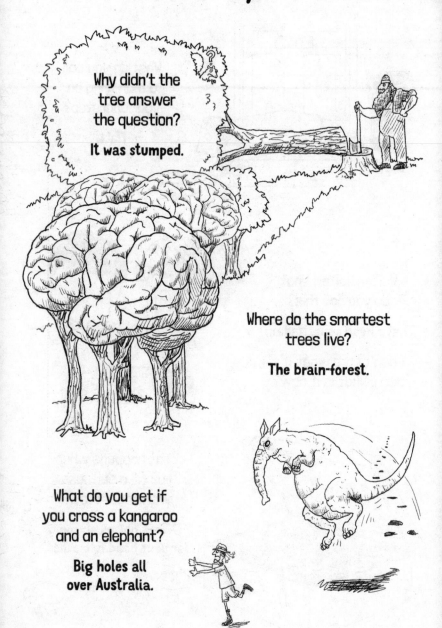

Why didn't the tree answer the question?

It was stumped.

Where do the smartest trees live?

The brain-forest.

What do you get if you cross a kangaroo and an elephant?

Big holes all over Australia.

What do you
call a rich elf?

Welfy.

What do you get when you
cross a cocker spaniel, a
poodle and a rooster?

A cocker-poodle-doo.

What do you call
two bananas?

A pair of slippers.

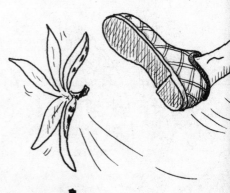

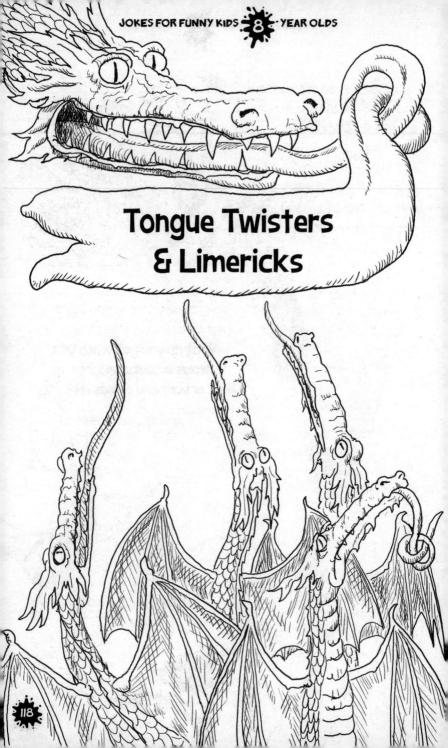

Tongue Twisters & Limericks

Peter Piper picked a
peck of pickled peppers.
A peck of pickled peppers
Peter Piper picked.
If Peter Piper picked a
peck of pickled peppers,
where's the peck of pickled
peppers Peter Piper picked?

There was an old man from Peru,
who dreamed he was
eating his shoe.
He woke in the night,
with a terrible fright,
to find out it was
perfectly true.

If a dog
chews shoes,
which shoes does
it choose?

The big black bug bit
the big black bear,
but the big black bear
bit the big black bug back.

There was a young
man from Bengal,
who went to a
masquerade ball.
He dressed, just for fun,
as a hamburger bun,
and a dog ate him up
in the hall.

Fuzzy wuzzy was a bear,
Fuzzy wuzzy had no hair.
So really, fuzzy wuzzy wasn't
very fuzzy, was he?

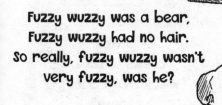

I wish to wash my
Irish wristwatch.

A skunk sat on a stump and thunk the stump stunk,
but the stump thunk the skunk stunk.

How much wood would a woodchuck chuck
if a woodchuck could chuck wood?
He would chuck, he would, as much as he could,
and chuck as much wood, as a woodchuck would
if a woodchuck could chuck wood.

I saw Susie sitting
in a shoe shine shop
Where she shines, she sits,
and where she sits,
she shines.

The great Greek grape
growers grow great
Greek grapes.

Six thick thistle
sticks are six
sticks thick.

There was a young schoolboy from Rye,
who was baked by mistake in a pie.
To his mother's disgust,
he emerged through the crust,
and exclaimed, with a yawn, "Where am I?"

Leaping lizards like
to lick lovely lemon
lollipops for lunch.

Betty Botter had some butter,
"But," she said, "this butter's bitter.
If I bake this bitter butter,
it would make my batter bitter.
But a bit of better butter –
that would make my batter better."

One day I went to the zoo,
for I wanted to see the old gnu.
But the old gnu was dead,
and the new gnu, they said,
was too new of a gnu to view.

She sells sea shells by the seashore.
The shells she sells are surely seashells.
So if she sells shells on the seashore,
I'm sure she sells seashore shells.

Fresh fried fish,
fish fresh fried,
fried fish fresh,
fish fried fresh.

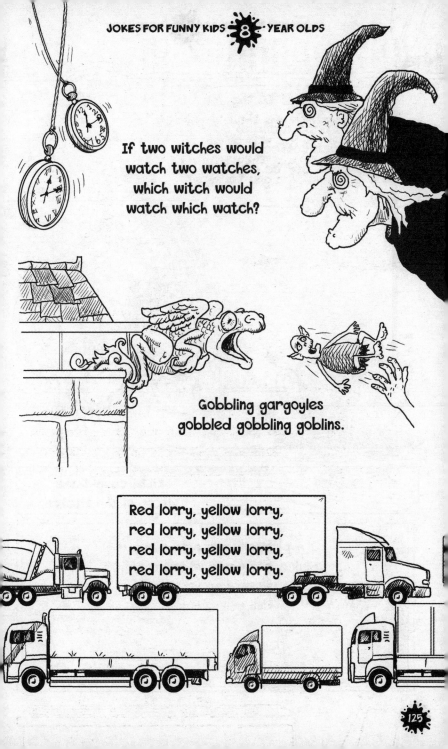

If two witches would watch two watches, which witch would watch which watch?

Gobbling gargoyles gobbled gobbling goblins.

Red lorry, yellow lorry,
red lorry, yellow lorry,
red lorry, yellow lorry,
red lorry, yellow lorry.

Give papa a cup of proper coffee in a copper coffee cup.

Kitty caught the kitten in the kitchen.

A pleasant place to place a plaice is a place where a plaice is pleased to be placed.

There once were two
cats from Kilkenny.
Each thought that was
one cat too many,
so they started to fight
and to scratch and to bite.
Now, instead of two cats,
there aren't any.

Whether the weather be fine,
or whether the weather be not,
whether the weather be cold,
or whether the weather be hot,
we'll weather the weather,
whatever the weather,
whether we like it or not.

The sixth sick shepherd's
sixth sheep's sick.